August 2022

"The midwife of change? An exploration of the effects of the COVID-19 Pandemic on degrowth and green growth narratives"

Abstract

My research is an exploration into the effects of the COVID-19 pandemic on the development of the 'Degrowth' and 'Green growth' narratives. The research analyses the positioning that the two theories have been able to gain prior to the pandemic, researching the lenses of crises that have brought about their progress. This sees the discussion of the growing climate/ environmental crises, the 2008 financial crisis, and the decline of neoliberal hegemony that is linked to these events. This provides a firm basis on which to compare their progress and position during and beginning of post-pandemic, where I will find that the radical ideas were either corroborated by the pandemic, with case studies demonstrating the possibility for their fruitfulness, or contradicted by the ongoings of the COVID years. The research found that the pandemic operated as a substantial catalytic event for both theories, in its capacity to produce profound societal change. Ultimately it provided mobility for both theories and opened discursive space for alternatives due its significant undermining of the systems of the status quo, such as excessive production/consumption, globalisation, and neoliberalism. The green growth movement, as it did prior to the pandemic, has remained and grown in the mainstream owing to its lack of criticism of growthism, and dominates the rhetoric of recovery. Despite the pandemic illuminating the shortcomings and environmental populism of the theory, its tenets afford it the support of powerful actors. The degrowth movement has observed a growth in its feasibility, due to the enactment of policy proposals aligned with its interests, and growth in support from grassroots sectors. However, the short-term benefits for the degrowth narrative, which saw emissions decline heavily, have been outweighed by the substantial weight of the recovery rhetoric. This has been a sharp rise in emissions since the initial lockdown due to a growth-based rebound, with investment returning to pollutant industries. The pandemic does not appear to be the midwife of change, as it seems the outcome of the 2008 crisis with a return to excessive growthism to facilitate recovery is being pursued, albeit under a green guise and environmental populism. However, the pandemic has done more for the degrowth movement than any previous crisis and has provided a peak behind the veil of economic dogma for many people, illuminating the capacity for a well-being, convivial socio-economic revolution.

Table of Contents

1. Introduction

The COVID-19 pandemic, which started to spread around December 2019, has been one of the most significant and disruptive events of recent human history (GOV, 2020). The spread of the virus globally has had profound impacts on the functioning of global systems, societies and the normal habits of humanity, with attempts to slow the spread resulting in global policies which limited human interaction, travel and the functioning of economic mechanisms. While being a global health crisis, the pandemic has exhibited far more than this and has served to provide insights into the social, economic and environmental state of the planet. Due to its disruptions to the traditional hegemonic systems of the world, it has been able to provide both the discursive space and experimental policy platform through which alternative socio-economic theories have been able to gain ground. Such alternative theories to the status quo have been presented as solutions and conducive to fostering a paradigm which will placate the growing climate crisis and planetary degradation, which is one of the underlying lenses of crisis that is referred to in this paper.

The climate crisis in which the world finds itself, has demonstrably been 'impacting human lives and health in a variety of ways. It threatens the essential ingredients of good health – clean air, safe drinking water, nutritious food supply and safe shelter – and has the potential to undermine decades of progress in global health' (WHO, 2019). The extent of climate change has progressed to a severe extent, where humanity affects the planet to an unprecedented level known as the Anthropogenic era, being the 'unofficial unit of geologic time, used to describe the most recent period in Earth's history when human activity started to have a significant impact on the planet's climate and ecosystems' (National Geographic Society, 2022). This context of crisis had been instrumental in bringing about the proposals for alternative policy solutions and systemic changes which seek to diminish the impact of humanity on the planet, resulting initially in the birth of the sustainable development movement which is "development that meets the needs of the present, without compromising the ability of future generations to meet their own needs." (Sustainable development commission, 2019) and later the degrowth and green growth movements.

The theories in question differ fundamentally in their approach to the climate crisis, with degrowth scholars approaching the issue as a systemic one which must tackle social, economic, and democratic issues in order to produce transformative change of excessive consumption and production habits which are the driving force of climate change, in their opinion. Importantly, degrowth views the forces of the status quo as being problematic, namely neoliberalism and globalisation which facilitate the environment for dangerous and unlimited levels of economic growth at the expense of the environment. The problem lies, for this movement, in the culture of growthism which they suggest is incompatible with a healthy planet. Contrastingly, green growth offers a technocratic solution to the climate crisis by offering investment in green technology and jobs to produce a continually growing economy that is decoupled from producing greenhouse gas (GHG) emissions. In this capacity, future growth is a solution to the climate crisis, not the cause.

This research situates the position of degrowth and green growth narratives within further themes of crisis, being the supposed decline of neoliberalism and globalisation and a continual reference to the 2008 financial crisis as a comparative crisis affecting calls for alternatives. Neoliberalism has been referred to as a free market system, advocating for little government intervention and 'its belief in sustained economic growth as the means to achieve human progress' (Smith, 2018). Globalisation can be defined as 'the spread of the flow of financial products, goods, technology, information, and jobs across national borders and cultures. In economic terms, it describes an interdependence of nations around the globe fostered through free trade' (Fernando, 2022). This represents an important lens of change in the research, where the supposed decline of neoliberalism and globalisation has been hyper-imposed throughout the pandemic, and the theories in question both take separate stances on the issue. The development of degrowth and green growth narratives before and during the pandemic, though, has been shaped by the shifts in the power of the dominant socio-economic order, and thus is an important frame of reference as it has implications for the ability of the narratives to achieve progress. In addition to this, the research explores the 2008 financial crisis as a point of comparison due to its similarities, producing environmental benefits due to economic slowdown, changes in lifestyles and representing a potentially catalytic moment for systemic change. Despite the opportunity of the crisis to take advantage of a reduction in emissions, it ultimately resulted in a rebound to high levels of pollution and environmental degradation. This current crisis will be observed in its capacity either to reproduce this effect or learn from the past.

What progress is made will indicate how likely lessons are to be learned from 2008, how resilient existing systems are to shock and likelihood to rebound, what policies are really possible, and how open society is to systemic change. This research is significant in that it brings together multiple lenses of crisis to analyse how the socio-economic alternatives achieve progress in the wake of a global health crisis. The pandemic acts as a microcosmic version of the development of climate change, showing us which sort of changes are possible, how willing people are to change, and how strong the status quo is, which in turn illuminates the progress made and space available for alternative solutions to climate change.

The research will begin by outlining the definitional space and arguments made offered by the degrowth and green growth narratives, outlining how much progress and success they had made prior to the pandemic. Scholarly arguments, policy support and mainstream prevalence will all be assessed in order to establish a position with which to compare the COVID-19 pandemic. This debate will be situated within the crises of climate change, declining neoliberalism and globalisation and the importance of the 2008 financial crisis as the potential catalysing effect that crises can have. Following this the research will explore the impacts of the pandemic on society, how changes in consumption and production, investment, behaviour, and the environmental impacts have caused shifts in the narratives. This will be followed by conclusive remarks summarising the progress made by degrowth and green growth narratives, and how their progress is indicative of the nature of the recovery and change which will manifest.

2. Methodology

The methodological basis of this paper will take the form of a long literature review and continual analysis throughout the paper. I will use the available secondary literature which has been produced on the topics of degrowth and green growth by academics, leading institutions, news organisations and professionals. Using this material, I will outline the positionality of the theories that had existed prior to the COVID-19 pandemic, reviewing the arguments of scholars and evidence of their progress to map out a point whereby a comparison with the pandemic era can be made. This second section of literature will occupy a comparative position in which inferences are able to be drawn where the progress of the narratives in question will be analysable. Ultimately the literature will provide the evidence to effectively draw conclusion on the effects of the paradigm of the pandemic on the development of socio-economic alternatives to the status quo. The research aims of the project are to establish the narrative positions of the degrowth and green growth movements prior to the pandemic, exploring the arguments and cases for them. The project aims to establish whether COVID has advanced these narratives, and whether the context of crisis has created an environment more favourable to the theories, and whether the pandemic will produce significant change which seeks to combat climate change in comparison to the 2008 financial crisis.

3. Degrowth pre-pandemic

3.1 How has degrowth been defined?

The establishment of the degrowth movement may be attributed to the work of Serge Latouche. His work came to prominence in the growing dissatisfaction that was felt towards the paradigm of 'sustainable development' which achieved dominance before the millennium. The trajectory of his conceptions was built in the attempt to displace hegemonic narratives that 'infinite economic growth' was the 'one way future for the whole of humanity' and that growth and improvement are mutually inclusive terminology (Mastini, 2017). Degrowth can be considered a response to dominant indicators such growth in Gross Domestic Product (GDP), being the 'total monetary or market value of all the finished goods and services produced within a country's borders in a specific time period' which measure the increases in the productive capacities of economies (Fernando, 2022). This has been seen as a blunt policy goal with possibly negative social and environmental effects, while arguing that there is an entrenched acceptance that capitalist society which centres around growth is the ultimate end of history and desirable economic pursuit, which we may see in the works of theorists like Fukuyama. Degrowth proposals debate the wide held thought of theorists such as Fukuyama that we exist at the 'end of history' in which there is no alternative to the dominance of capitalist liberal democracies, which have supposedly proven themselves to be the most successful political and economic ideologies of history having surpassed the collapse of the Soviet Union (Fukuyama, 1989). Here we see the crux of degrowth, which is a challenge to the supremacy of the growthist narrative and its rejection of all alternatives.

Degrowth, for Kallis, represents an attempt to grapple the externalities that are encountered through perpetual material growth. In this scenario we see that the increasing use of matter and energy by societies is 'responsible for the adverse climate and ecological effects' that are experienced the continual pushing of the planetary limits by economic growth (Kallis et al, 2020). This premise leads to a central tenet of degrowth theory, that economies should pursue a reduction in material throughput in order to achieve the desired reductions in planetary damage (Perkins, 2019). Not only does the theory push for 'throughput decline' with a reduction in the material output and resource use of economies, but further a 'cultural and institutional decolonisation from economism and the religion of growth' that is deeply entrenched In public attitudes and policy (Kallis, 2011). The sustainability of degrowth is emphasised in that it should result in 'social sustainability' and the 'equitable reduction of societies throughput' being the materials and energy a society extracts, processes, transports and distributes and returns back to the environment as waste' (Kallis, 2011). This position of degrowth is twofold in that it supposes to challenge the economic system based on tangible reductions in the economic activity as well as cultural transformations away from dominant economic and political dogma. This demonstrates the radical position that the theory holds situated within the contemporary power of growthism, which will be discussed (Kallis, 2011).

This is a definitional attempt that is supported by other degrowth scholars. Similarly, there is a perception from others that degrowth exists to tackle a plurality of problems. Schneider frames degrowth as a conception which tackles the problems of an environmental, social and economic nature. To this end they propose to reduce the "collective capacity to acquire and use physical resources" (Schneider et al, 2010). This, he argues, should result in an "an equitable downscaling of production and consumption… increases human well-being and enhances ecological conditions at the local and global level, in the short and long term" (Schneider et al, 2010). The importance of this conceptual offering, while agreeing with other scholars, is that it represents the multifaceted nature of degrowth in its problem and solution perception. Degrowth represents, according to Schneider, the acceptance that in order to solve problems of an environmental nature through means of the economy that we must engage with social issues, and that all of these issues are deeply connected. This view is supported by the scale of interdisciplinary academics involved in the degrowth debate, where we have seen scholars of 'culturalist' backgrounds such as anthropologists, social policy scholars, economists, and environmental academics (Schneider et al, 2010). The presence of such variety in the debate demonstrated that beyond economic concerns, the degrowth debate grapples with a plurality of issues in tandem in which they help solve one another.

3.1 How has degrowth experienced development?

To examine the development of the degrowth narrative and the discursive space it occupies we must explore the historical traces and causal factors that have contributed to their arguments. There are a plethora of phenomena, events and systems that have enabled degrowth to emerge as a concept that occupies a critical position of the status quo. The urgency and significance of the current environmental crisis threatening the planet, as discussed in the introduction, has been brought forth in the Anthropocene. In response to the existential developments of planetary decline, degrowth scholars and professionals attribute the phenomenon to the externalities of excessive consumption and production. Steffen discusses that this is in response to the failure of sustainable development and climate mitigation since the 1980s, where the crossing of 4/9 established planetary boundaries had already occurred (Asara et al, 2015). These infringements upon the limits of the planet are the result 'imperial mode of living' of the global north it is argued, where the culture of consumption has evolved with the 'method of personal identity' according to Hamilton (Schneider, 2010). Kallis supports this view in their assessment of consumer identity being an integral element of perpetuating growthist fetish on a personal level, which conditions us into believing that more is better on a larger level (Kallis et al, 2020), and is aided heavily by the power of the marketing industry, who have the influence to ensure demand continues to rise (Silva, 2020). To understand the position of degrowth and the entrenchment of growthism, however, we must under the political and social forces that have given rise to it.

The fixation and persistence of growthism as the dominant framework through the guise of sustainable development has taken place under the political and economic pre-eminence of the neoliberal system. The neoliberal system is characterised by its push for free-market capitalism, limited government intervention and is often framed in 'terms of its belief in sustained economic growth as the means to achieve human progress' (Smith, 2018). This movement, which champions growthism, reached mainstream prominence in the 1980s under the premierships of Ronald Reagan and Margaret Thatcher, and allowed the free-market obsession with growthism at all costs to achieve political capture. We can exhibit the capture of politics by neoliberal concepts through the quote from Margaret Thatcher, claiming that her greatest achievement was "Tony Blair and New Labour. We forced our opponents to change their minds", showing a move towards hegemonic status of growth dominated politics and economics (Bregman, 2020). The dominance of this system, as discussed in degrowth literature, was instrumental in bringing about crises of both and environmental nature, with the pushing of planetary boundaries, and social nature which will be discussed in the context of the 2008 financial crisis.

The 2008 financial crisis is significant in the context of the degrowth movement and debate, this is due to it demonstrating that reckless pursuit of limitless growth comes at a cost, and ultimately such an economy caters towards the narrow interests of few and not the wellbeing of the majority. Bregman discusses that, despite at first appearing to be a peek behind the veil of neoliberalism, the growthist system was able to reassert itself in the aftermath of the crisis. The result was huge bailouts to 'save the free market', and contrastingly the masses faced rapidly rising inequality and cuts to public services (Bregman, 2020). This demonstrates the systemic neglect of wellbeing that has been discussed, where the endless pursuit of growth has in this case not resulted in rises in happiness and improvement, but rather illustrates that growth benefits a select few.

The financial crisis, however, took place during a trajectory of changing attitudes where we see that the degrowth narrative was mirrored by societal transformations. This is visible in the rise of alternative indicators to GDP and its embracement in the mainstream. GDP, it is posited by Gertney, has been subject to a shift where we now see a 'proliferation of new measures that are available to all' which serves to challenge the hegemonic framing of prosperity (Gertney, 2010). He further argues that this 'easy access to information' will shift the debate and result in changing perceptions on well-being, where previous systems equated more consumption with more happiness we are now in an epoch where there a new ways of evaluating national progress which opens up discursive space for policy (Gertney, 2010). The solidification of this, and arguably representing the agreement with some of degrowths tenets, is the mainstream representation of alternative indicators. In 2009 French President Sarkozy established a panel to 'identify the limits of GDP as an indicator of economic performance and social progress' and similarly in 2010 British Prime Minister David Cameron declared that "there is more to life than money and it's time we focussed not just on GDP but on GWP – general well-being" (Ferguson, 2014). However, Silva discusses the progress of such indicators, arguing that although the Easterlin Paradox of GDP has been exposed, which tells us that 'additional increases in GDP do not reflect in increased happiness after reaching a level of income', we still observe that GDP and importantly growthism is still the hegemonic indicator and the Human Development Index (HDI) is one of few genuine attempts at weakening (Silva, 2020). This would serve to argue that the degrowth movement, although has seen tokenistic movements towards achieving progress in the mainstream, has not seized sufficient tangible progress. The apparent lack of tangibility, however, is contradicted by the change in perception in some countries, for example we see in the case of the UK and Australia

that '1/5th of the population have voluntarily reduced their income and consumption to spend more time with their family and friends' (Schneider, 2010). This represents a more grassroots behavioural change, with a move towards post-materialism livelihoods that do not equate growth and increased consumption with well-being and happiness. This is complementary to the narrative of degrowth.

A significant component to the narrative of Degrowth is that were in intersects with the development of neoliberalism. The attitudes that have been shaped over history by dominant socio-economic ideology demonstrate a natural scepticism to alternatives which question growth, for example of a study taken regarding degrowth '32 % of sample associated term with 'moving backwards' and 43% chose it as the least appealing term of 5' (Tomaselli et al, 2021). This, it is argued by some, is due to a characteristic of neoliberalism where economic debate is kept out of the remit of public debate, which is demonstrated by the absence of public knowledge about economic alternatives.

Chomsky makes the point that 'growth and guiding economic philosophy has been demonstrably off bounds to the masses, remaining the exclusive remit of the political and corporate elite' (Chomsky, 2011). This brings the focus to the arguments made by degrowth proponents that the solving of environmental and social crises necessitates the 'decentralising and deepening of democratic institutions and repoliticising the economy' as an arena of public debate (Schneider, 2010). The decline of neoliberalism, however, is argued by many to be in process, and tangibly culminated in the externalities of the 2008 financial crisis. As well as this, the so called 'tribune of capitalism' the Financial Times has become more critical of the system, pushing for governments to have a 'more active role in the economy' and give greater attention to 'redistribution', representing a challenge from one of its foremost supporters (Bregman, 2020). This, accompanied with the development of alternative indicators and the financial crisis, represents a critical juncture in the hegemony of neoliberalism, and the scope for mobility with alternatives.

3.2 Degrowth policy discussion

Proponents of degrowth propose a number of policies in order to achieve their environmental and social objectives, many of these presented prior to the COVID-19 pandemic. Kallis refers to the prominent policies of Universal Basic Income as well as a reduction in the working hours of the week, this he argues would have the effect of producing positive environment and social externalities due to a reduction in pollution (Kallis et al, 2020). The argument for this has been supported by modelling predictions produced, for example the Canada model saw that where 'GDP per person gradually reduced by 50% over 30 years – with offsetting policies such as work-sharing, redistributive income transfers' it resulted in GHG reductions of 80% (Cassidy, 2020). In addition to this, Everingham discusses that the degrowth movement recommends the shortening of global supply chains and the relocation of production, i.e. a counter movement against the developed forces of globalisation and neoliberalism which have extended production and consumption to a level of unprecedented global interconnectedness (Everingham and Chassagne, 2020). An example of degrowth in action was exhibitable in Barcelona, where a semi-autonomous, collective system squat had formed (Schneider, 2010). What this example was able to demonstrate for the movement was that, when the necessary collective action is taken, it is possible to achieve an alternative system which saw 'energy use and material per person far below the average of the area' in an environment with a commonly agreed lifestyle emphasising wellbeing (Schneider, 2010). These policies represent the progress made in the degrowth movement in proposing tangible solutions, rather than pure rhetorical critique of the status quo. However, the theory and its proposals are vulnerable to critique which will be discussed next.

3.3 Degrowth critiques

One of the fundamental critiques against the progress of degrowth is through pointing at the successes of the status quo and growthist dominance. For many sceptics, the alleged triumph of capitalism and economic growth can be best seen in the success seen in India and China. The growing end to extreme poverty in this region is attributed to the fact that they have 'grown their way out of poverty' (Rashid et al, 2021). The growth has come as a result of 'integration with global capitalist economies', embracing the economic culture of the west, culminating in the lifting of millions out of poverty and the emergence of a new affluent middle class in those countries (Cassidy, 2020). So, it is put by these scholars that to have denied India and China this opportunity may have seen a continuation of the extreme poverty conditions that were so prevalent prior to their development, which undermines degrowth as a strategy to achieve social progress alongside environmental benefits. This argument is also supported by the 'kicking away the ladder' narrative (Joon-Chang, 2002), which critiques western hypocrisy in the face of scholarly and professional calls for system change in the developing world, when countries like the US and UK were free to pursue development strategies without interference (Rashid et al, 2021). This certainly represents a difference in standards when it comes to development, with degrowth potentially representing a hypocritical position if exerted on developing countries.

However, this point is countered by some scholars who see that the necessity for the developing world to stray from the path set by the west is essential in producing the environmental outcomes that are essential for planetary protection. Latouche argues that they should 'aim not for development but for disentanglement... Southern countries need to escape their economic and cultural dependence on the north and rediscover their own histories' and that ultimately the outrage at overconsumption should be a guiding principle of future development (Foster, 2011). This is based on the impossibility theorem, which posits that a 'us stile high mass consumption economy for a world of 4 billion people is impossible' (Foster, 2011). This represents a defence of degrowth through the extent to which overconsumption is highly detrimental to the environment and unable to be replicated on a larger scale, particularly at this juncture of the climate crisis.

Another critique and barrier to the progress of degrowth, for some academics, is how current habits and behaviours are so deeply entrenched in the culture of society that it would be impossible to produce the change in lifestyles that degrowth proposes. Koch recognises that there exists concern among current generations that there will be negative implications for wellbeing in a degrowth paradigm (Büchs and Koch, 2019). Kallis similarly discusses the 'lock in' factor of lifestyle as representing a substantial barrier to degrowth (Kallis, 2011), where consumption is a 'method of personal identity' and greater consumption is fetishized (Schneider, 2010). This signifies the strength of existing systems in entrenching habits and undermining alternatives and presents a case that fundamental change may not be possible. This position, however, is vulnerable through the example of historical crises facilitating substantial change. For example, the Second World War saw a transformation of the US economy, resulting in 'reasonable planned democratic economy redistributing surpluses from private consumption to public goods' and importantly 'conspicuous consumption became socially ostracised' (Kallis, 2011). This is hugely significant in that crises can present the opportunity to produce catalytic change, and further that people can adapt their lifestyles in the face of a common purpose. Such adaptability is the crux of degrowth fervour, which is said to be essential in combatting excessive lifestyles and climate change.

4. Green growth

This section will introduce the concept of green growth to the debate, being a proposal to placate the increasingly indiscrete planetary degradations and environmental instability, discussing the fundamental attributes of the concept and explore the progress the narrative had made prior to the COVID-19 pandemic. Firstly, the section will begin with a summary of what green growth is and what it proposes as the means by which to solve environmental issues. Next, I will discuss the historical lineage of the theory, seeking to answer how the concept emerged and from which sectors/academic fields it is supported by. The significance of the theory will be analysed in it terms of the sort of solutions it offers, and these in turn will be compared with the offerings of the degrowth movement. Comparisons discussed between the degrowth and green growth movement should illuminate key similarities and differences in their diagnostics of sources and solutions to environmental issues, or indeed related issues. This is important in answering the key research question of how COVID-19 has impacted the narratives of these theories, as we are able to analyse how their arguments and positions progressed or were discredited during the pandemic compared to prior.

4.1 How has green growth been defined?

The green growth movement is one that can be characterised by a number of constituent elements. It is argued that green growth has come to be the 'current dominant strategy of mainstream economists and policy makers to address climate change' and progressed to have a 'stronger support base than sustainable development', but how has this change been achieved? The proponents of the movement elect that the most effective and least disruptive solution to the environmental crises is to pursue incremental change that is 'based on mainly market led or market confirmed processes and induced technological change' (Kallis et al, 2020). This undertaking, Wells argues, is 'likely to lead to a net decline in ecological burdens' though 'greater regulation' and 'emergent technology' (Wells et al, 2020). Cassidy discusses this further, engaging with arguments that granted the correct policy measures and 'technological progress' then perpetual growth should be possible (Cassidy, 2020). The 2018 Global Commission on the Economy and Climate reinforce this view of green growth advocates by stressing that 'growth is driven by the interaction between rapid technological innovation, sustainable infrastructure investment, and increased resource productivity' which can facilitate sustainable growth (Cassidy, 2020). The harnessing of continuous technological improvement, it is argued, is to achieve the 'absolute decoupling' of GDP from greenhouse gas (GHG) emissions in order to sustain growth and mitigate the harmful impact of emissions (Hickel and Kallis, 2019). This literature highlights the central significance that investment and technological advancements play in green growth proposals, demonstrating its technocratic, rather than systemic, approach to environmental issues.

Kallis recognises the view within green growth theorisations that this endeavour necessitates being led by the private sector and innovative, profit-led processes, in which 'growth remains the central means to enable ongoing socio-economic transformation' (Kallis et al, 2020). This is a view offered, however, by a degrowth scholar and arguably presents a fatalist case, dismissing its scope by attributing it centrally to the dangers of profiteering, that some other academics or professionals may disagree with. Others, for example, frame green growth as being a managed transition that seeks to bring public and private sectors together, with companies bringing 'resources, skills and competencies' to produce technocratic and innovative solutions to the problem of climate change and alongside 'strong state regulation for environmental and other reasons' which 'is beneficial for companies' (Wells et al, 2020). Although the offerings of these literature differ in their appreciation of the scope of green growth, with its capacity to involve more than just the private sector, there is a fundamental recognition that it is a gradual process which seeks to utilise technological innovation and investment to solve environmental issues. Further in the literature, however, is the foundational acceptance that growth remains an unproblematic concept, where economic growth 'which also achieves significant environmental protection' is desirable, and rather presents itself as conducive to a solution (Ferguson, 2014). This illustrates that no matter the extent to which public and private actors contribute to green growth, that growth in itself is not viewed as conducive to environmental degradation, but rather it is harmful and unregulated growth.

4.2 How has the narrative experienced development?

The green growth narrative, while displacing the position of sustainable development, has allowed itself to achieve support from powerful and influential actors. We can exhibit this in the extent to which dominant institutions have transformed and begun to champion the movement as a necessary solution. For example, the Organisation for Economic Co-operation and Development (OECD), who recognise the potentiality for green growth to come forth through 'framework conditions that mutually reinforce economic growth and the conservation of natural capital', while recognising that existing growth dynamics have breached 'planetary boundaries' (Ferguson, 2014). Similarly, we are able to view an institutional extension of this belief through the International Monetary Fund (IMF), who have taken the position that 'inclusive green growth' which is 'efficient in its use of natural resources' and 'clean in that it minimises pollution and environmental impacts' will be able to placate the previous dangerous levels of growth which have come 'largely at the expense of the environment' (Ferguson, 2014). And as Ferguson refers to as perhaps the most 'promising' backing, we see that the United Nations Environmental Programme (UNEP) critiques the existing economic system as being the result of a 'gross misallocation of capital' which manifests in the form of 'excessive resource depletion' which poses the risk of having temporal challenges for the wellbeing of current and future generations (Ferguson, 2014).

Here, it is recognised that among leading financial and environmental institutions that the theory of green growth has been embraced. It has been done so on the basis of a critique of the dangers of excessive growth and an acceptance that an efficient level of growth is achievable. This represents a clear move away from conventional growth, but nonetheless an appreciation that 'continued economic expansion is compatible with our planet's ecology' (Hickel and Kallis, 2019). We may place this in the wider context of world leaders denouncing traditional mechanisms. This was visible in the statements made by Sarkozy and Cameron which situate green growth narratives equally in the trajectory of reformulation surrounding what purpose an economy should serve and what the parameters of prosperity are. The development of alternative measures of progress is a coincident occurrence alongside the development of green growth narratives, with conventional indicators being challenged. However, it still emphasises that the best way to achieve success in this new prosperity valuation is through the traditional mechanism of growth, and a belief that GDP growth is still able to be utilised, pursued, and most importantly decoupled from detrimental environmental impacts. Although green growth and degrowth intersect and capitalise on such shifts in opinion, they both disagree on the means to achieve this and ultimately desired goals such as wellbeing.

The development of the green growth narrative, as an economic alternative, has been able to achieve significant success in comparison to others, most notably degrowth. We have seen that it has achieved mainstream prominence in a number of leading international institutions. This is hugely important, and the propensity of green growth to achieve greater progress over other proposals must be analysed. It is argued that this is ultimately because the theory embraces growthism which acts to preserves the architecture of the status quo. Ferguson argues that by avoiding the 'Achilles heel' of environmental politics, which is its criticism of economic growth, that it resultantly benefits from significant corporate, political and institutional backing, giving the movement greater ability to achieve discursive power and narrative progress (Ferguson, 2014). This characteristic lack of substantial challenge to hegemonic economic ideas presents the movement with a 'strategic merit' by 'turning a negative debate about costly constraints into a narrative about opportunity' in which the supposed benefits of economic growth continue (Bowen and Fankhauser, 2011). This demonstrates the strengths in the proliferation of the green growth narrative, as rather than occupying a position of radical critique, it rather presents transformative potential in its ability to 'rearticulate existing growth discourses subversively' (Ferguson, 2014). This illuminates the position significantly of green growth in the pre-covid years, allowing insight into what has enabled it to achieve prominence in the mainstream. However, the theory, due to simply adapting existing structures, is susceptible to critique based on how much fundamental change it can resultantly bring about which will be discussed next.

4.3 Critiques of green growth

The green growth movement, having made notable progress in its endorsement, has also found itself receiving criticism, which undermine the theories' ability to offer a feasible response to environmental degradation. Firstly, one of the key tenets of green growth, being that it is possible to decouple resource use and carbon emissions from economic growth, has come increasingly under fire. Many scholars subscribe to this view, where we see Rashid electing that 'there is no evidence that resource use can be decoupled from growth' and rather we would see that 'extraction rates would only increase' (Rashid et al, 2021) as well as Ferguson who explores the lack of relevant evidence of decoupling success. He makes the point that in a growing economy 'absolute decoupling is likely to remain elusive' (Ferguson, 2014). This represents fundamental academic opposition to one of its key arguments. However, some literature proposes that it is able to be countered, for example environmental economists Bowen and Hepburn insist that 'by 2050' absolute decoupling may appear "to have been a relatively easy challenge" due to 'scientific research into green technology' (Bowen and Hepburn, 2014). Asara similarly recognises that there is some evidence of relative decoupling achieving success with 'world GDP rising faster than carbon dioxide emissions over the last 18 years', however they go on to discuss that absolute decoupling of resource use has not occurred (Asara et al, 2015). Demonstrably, the decoupling paradigm of degrowth is vulnerable to criticism which has undermined its ability to appeal to a greater plurality of actors and scholars as there is lack of evidence for one of its fundamental tenets. The arguments made against this are substantiated, we may say, through the failure of green growth to achieve its supposed aims. Wells discusses that there been 'growing perception that green growth was failing to deliver the required pace and scale of carbon-emissions reductions at national or international level', and so comparisons must be drawn with the sustainable development movement which exhibited similar negative perception owing to its lack of tangible progress (Wells, 2020). Despite being the successor and alleged solution to the shortcomings of sustainable development, green growth risks reproducing its failings.

The propensity for failure faced by the green growth is one characterised by the means it chooses to placate a reduction in harmful emissions, where the point is made that the theory is overly ambitious. In order to achieve the supposed decoupling, which is central to green growth, the conception finds itself heavily reliant on perpetual innovation capacity of growthist market systems to consistently balance out increasing consumption and production of human populations. Foster makes the point that although some elect that we are in the midst of a 'green industrial revolution' creating constant progress (Ferguson, 2014), ultimately 'the promise of green technology has proven false' (Foster, 2011). The slow achievement of carbon-emission reductions is attributed by some scholars to the Jevons Paradox, which puts that the emphasis on efficiency will not result in conservation but rather produces an oxymoron whereby 'decreased resource requirements lead to lower costs' which will lead to a rebound in consumption and more growth (Kallis). Essentially, for Kallis, this represents an immutable part and issue with growthism, that 'increasing productivity frees up resources that are invested to provide yet more growth', and so the same logic that has contributed towards rising emissions is reproduced (Kallis, 2015). Importantly, it is predicted that by the end of the century we may see global average temperatures 3-6 degrees above pre-industrial levels (OECD, 2012). It must be said that the reliance on perpetual future innovation represents a gamble, which within the current lens of existential environmental crisis may prove to lack necessary urgency. This raises the question then, of whether green growth promises more than it delivers.

The aforementioned criticisms are significant in that they leave green growth vulnerable to accusations of environmental populism, i.e., being too good to be true (Antal and Van Den Bergh, 2014). Literature which problematises the foundation of decoupling and those which highlight the slow progress in reducing emissions that has resulted would corroborate these arguments. In addition to this, the premise that green growth represents environmental populism, some argue, is that it fails to challenge the status quo. Having discussed the progress and position of the narrative within institutions it is supported by hegemonic actors and interests, having succeeded the sustainable development movement, and for some scholars this is attributed to the fact that while 'they aim to influence the environmental impact of consumption, most approaches do not question existing patterns of living and consuming' (Bär, Jacob and Werland, 2011). This is indicative of the lack of disruptive capacity of green growth to change the status quo, and the undertakings of the movement during COVID-19 are of a similar nature.

This point may be linked to the earlier quote by the Financial Times and corroborates the trajectory which indicates the decline and crisis of neoliberalism. Although green growth perspectives can be strengthened by this, which agree with this view that the unregulated free market has caused problems and greater government role is needed with economic alternatives, it is still a theory that centres around the supremacy of growth in consumption and production. This as a system risk perpetuating the same logics, that growthism can be harnessed as a solution, that have allowed neo-liberal levels of consumption and production to cause planetary damage. It may be argued that this presents the opportunity to justify 'more of the same under a green disguise' (Schneider, 2010). This opens up green growth to criticisms that it lacks scope in its solutions and diagnosis of the causes of planetary degradation. The threat of this is very real, as exhibited with the slow progress of championed movements which adapt existing approaches, such as sustainable development, and the slow progress of green growth to bring the climate crisis to heel is evidence of this.

5. The COVID-19 pandemic

The purpose of this section is to illustrate the significance of the COVID-19 pandemic in producing changes in the positions of the Green Growth and Degrowth movements comparative to their pre-pandemic development. I will do this by exploring the constituent elements that have defined the pandemic, being the fundamental nature of it as health crisis that has induced change and adaptation at almost every level of society and the planet. Firstly, I will outline the impacts of the pandemic paradigm on the climate and progression of planetary pollution, which will provide a point of discussion on what the cause of this is and significance in terms of possible recovery mechanisms. Following this, the debate surrounding the opportunism of crises will be analysed with reference to previous crises, the importance of which demonstrating that the development of such movements as degrowth and green growth are highly susceptible to change in the environment of radical economic and social displacement. The impetus of crisis as a catalyst is significant and fundamental to the research aims of this project, which seeks to explore how such dynamics may accelerate or hinder proposals that seek to remedy the growing environmental externalities of emissions and pollution. Particular areas of concern relevant to the theories that have been exposed in the pandemic will be explored, such as changes in the nature of investment and fiscal recovery, the behavioural changes for the population, the redistribution of power and changes in globalised forces, and ultimately the debate on what sort of recovery should be pursued based on the lessons learned through the event. The framing of the recovery debate, and who is deciding what sort of recovery is achieved will be discussed also, and these developments will all be used as points of comparison with pre-pandemic narratives to map the changes in debate and support.

5.1 The significance of the crisis

The COVID-19 pandemic and global health crisis, it must be stated, has been one of the most significant international events of the century. However, it has proven itself to be far more than a health crisis, being multifaceted in its capacity to cause disruption. As the UN frame 'It is a human, economic and social crisis' (United Nations, 2020). The ability of COVID to prove so impactful across a plurality of sectors is due to its limitations on human contact and travel. In order to ensure health security across the world, we have seen that around 54% of the global population has been subject to a complete or partial lockdown (Kuzemko, 2020), having profound effects on the functioning of society and shifts in political capital and attention. This is seen in the travel section, for example, where there was a 'reduction of 503-607 million passengers in the first half of 2020' (Hepburn et al, 2020). What was observed during the pandemic, as a result of the measures enforced to ensure the protection of public health, were positive environmental outcomes within a short time frame. As early as April 2020, we saw that daily global CO2 emissions 'fell by 17%' compared to 2019, 'oil use saw a 25% fall in April 2020' and expectations were of an 8% overall drop of CO2 emissions in 2020, which would take the emission levels back 10 years (Kuzemko, 2020). However, this optimism would be overly ambitious, as the data demonstrated we rather saw that 'Global energy-related CO2 emissions were 2% higher in December 2020 than in the same month a year earlier' owing to 'economic recovery and a lack of clean energy policies' (IEA, 2022). This is important for the research into the impacts on the degrowth and green growth for respective reasons, which will be explored firstly looking at green growth investment.

5.2 The role of investment

The pandemic, as has been the case with previous crises, has opened the space for discussions regarding investment and fiscal recovery. The economic damage incurred throughout the pandemic saw that the global economy was 'expected to shrink by about 5.2% in 2020 as a result of the coronavirus pandemic' (Zumbrun, 2020) and ultimately resulted in a decline of world output of '4.3 per cent' (United Nations, 2021). This has catalysed the level of preventative investments taking place and targeted fiscal programmes in order to placate the externalities of economic downturn. However, this has contributed to the debate surrounding the nature of the recovery that should take place, and when it comes to investment the literature indicates a continuation of the dominance of green growth narratives, hegemonic power structures and concepts such as growthism

The paradigm of the pandemic, it seems, has created the ripe environment for inducing green investment, and resultantly serves to advance the position of the green growth narrative. According to some scholars, there is a general agreement 'regarding the job creating potential of a green recovery' and many posit that the 'green recovery would contribute to GDP' (Gusheva and De Gooyert, 2021). Leading international institutions such as the European Union have claimed that we should 'indeed hope for a green recovery', as well as the UK Prime Minister Boris Johnson promising a 'green recovery' which strives to 'drive economic recovery from coronavirus' (Bogojevic, 2020). Similarly, we have seen that the IMF (International Monetary Fund) has called for calls for fiscal policymakers to '"green" their response to this crisis to prevent one crisis leading to another', and that the 'depth of the crisis and the scope of the response' will 'shape societies for decades to come' (IMF, n.d.). This follows on from the trajectory that green growth was already following, however it must be said that it is now being framed with particular urgency and with more vigour by some agents such as the IMF in the context of the crisis. This narrational uptake visibly culminates in policy plans, as discussed by the European Union with proposals to invest around '\$200 billion' in green energy which will 'boost jobs and growth' (Smith, 2020). As well as this, we have seen Boris Johnson announce '£350 million' to 'cut emissions In heavy industry, space and transport' (Bogojevic, 2020) with a government briefing to Universities also planning to bring 'short-term high economic impact' (Imperial College London, 2020). Additionally, companies worth '\$2 trillion' collectively have called for a green growth recovery to the pandemic (Taherzadeh, 2020). This serves to bolster the dominance of green growth and represents its consolidation in the mainstream, with powerful actors, institutions and global leaders galvanising momentum for recovery based on green growth principles.

While green growth has seemingly been able to achieve bolstering in its financial and institutional backing, it has also found itself being vulnerable to more critique in the wake of the pandemic. The dangers of the current trajectory of green growth have been outlined by some, arguing that it is 'not merely unambitious but stands to delay, disrupt and distance from necessary social and ecological transformation' (Taherzadeh, 2020). This makes the point that green growth attempts are inadequate, and additionally it is argued that the 'instability borne from COVID-19 has afforded hegemonic systems a source of security and normalcy' (Taherzadeh, 2020). This is significant as it indicates the narrative suffering from critique, highlighting its failure to properly challenge established practices while producing little transformation. Other literature provides context in terms of previous crises, and how the paradigm of potential change in the recovery process has merely resulted in a return to normality. In past examples we have seen economic crises reducing the rise of emissions, such as 1979 where 'emissions growth fell by one-third', 1991 with the breakup of the Soviet Union saw another reduction by a third, and most recently the 2008 financial crisis where 'emissions growth halved to 1.6% per year over the next decade' (Hanna et al, 2020). Despite this 'opportunity' resulting in '15% of global stimulus funding' going into 'developing and deploying green technologies' (Hanna et al, 2020), what resulted was 'Global carbon dioxide emissions from fossil-fuel combustion and cement production grew 5.9% in 2010' which 'more than offset the 1.4% decrease in 2009' (Peters et al, 2011). This underscores the propensity for a 2008 style recovery with COVID-19, and how the potential for change has precedent for facilitating the exact same processes and even producing more pollution to make up for lost time. This exact problem is visible in the emissions produced from the Chinese recovery to the pandemic, where by May 2020 'Chinese pollution had already over-shot their pre-crisis levels', despite arguments of green growth dominating the mainstream (Kuzemko, 2020).

In terms of investment and change, it is argued that 'many of the main drivers of what happens next represent a *continuation* of processes that pre-date the pandemic', which has resulted in questions of 'whether or not there will be an *acceleration* of trends towards a more sustainable future, or whether the desire to protect existing jobs and incumbent industry will retard the momentum that was emerging in some countries under the banner of a 'green new deal' or 'green growth' – (Kuzemko, 2020). As has been shown with dominant rhetoric, green growth is achieving progress and maintains a flagship position in regard to COVID-19 recoveries, but arguments made pre-pandemic have been bolstered by the shortcomings of green growth during the crisis. Arguments that there have been more promises than tangible plans made by green growth proponents, such as those companies worth $2 trillion contribute to the critical line made pre-pandemic, that green growth relies too heavily on future promises and technological bailout and represents environmental populism. In this sense, the pandemic has the effect of exposing the shortcomings of green growth arguments. This viewpoint finds clout where a 'survey of experts on relative performance of fiscal recovery policies from covid-19 found only a handful would provide positive climate impact with non-promising an immediate effect' (Taherzadeh, 2020).

In addition to the lack of tangible progress made by green growth promises, there has been exhibited a resurgence in Brown investment, being the more pollutant and environmentally damaging. Since the start of the pandemic and through the recovery effort, we can see that high-carbon infrastructure projects and fossil fuel companies have been 'major beneficiaries' of stimulus measures (Taherzadeh, 2020). In the US alone there have been 'oil, coal and fracking companies in line to benefit from $750bn bond scheme' (Harvey, 2020), and in order to subsidise the aviation industry in Australia there was a relief scheme worth '$32 billion' (Hepburn et al, 2020). Not only has green growth raised questions over its validity, but it is being accompanied by investment in old damaging industries which is justified in the name of recovery. This creates parallels with the 2008 financial crisis, where we saw green investment rise but it ultimately doing little to slow the spiralling climate crisis. Furthermore, the crisis has illuminated stratification over the green growth movement, with the US and the EU separating over the level of commitment to a green recovery. Here it has been shown that while the EU has promised around the area of $200 billion to such a recovery, the US has instead adopted a relaxation of 'laws controlling pollution and standards for vehicle energy efficiently' and other policies (Hanna et al, 2020). This demonstrates a lack of uniformity on the green recovery in the face of the crisis, and perhaps even a step away from it in the case of the US. This presents a case that green growth either does not do enough on its own, or does not do enough to subvert the damaging forces of growthism which have reasserted themselves to support damaging industries. Instead, it presents the potentiality for COVID to justify a drastic return to pollutant systems in order to save jobs, putting environmental concerns momentarily out of the spotlight. This apprehension is expressed by France's ambassador to Canada, who observed "The fear is that because the economy has been so down, we will want recovery at any price" (McCarthy, 2020).

5.3 Decoupling

The impacts of COVID-19 for green growth, as well as illuminating the potential of its investment rhetoric, have also been seen in one of its fundamental arguments, that GDP growth and emissions are able to be successfully decoupled. It has been seen in the pandemic that due to the downturn in human activity that emissions have resultantly experienced a shift downwards. Evidence of the decline in consumption and production resulting in significant reductions in GHG emission serves to undermine one of the fundamental arguments of the green growth movement, that we were achieving the successful decoupling of growth and emissions. Helm discusses this, claiming that 'contrary to the claims that GDP and emissions have been decoupled, they have been highly correlated for most countries' (Helm, 2020). This is of significant damage to the success the narrative had been achieving during the pandemic, at least in terms of solidifying its mainstream position. Where previously there had been lack of significant evidence that decoupling was working, and achieving the necessary progress to combat climate change, this has been exemplified in blatant fashion in the pandemic and clearly not reached the levels its supporters had claimed. Through exposing a flaw in one of its fundamental arguments, this is particularly damaging to the validity of the green growth movement.

6. Degrowth elements of covid

6.1 Exposure of systemic failures

The COVID-19 pandemic, due to the profound impacts it produced globally, was able to serve as a barometer of the current systems that governed the world. Resultantly, the responses, shortcomings and successes have been judged in relation to the dominant economic, social and political apparatus that shape global affairs. Multiple scholars have discussed the capacity that the pandemic has held to disrupt and expose flaws in these systems, which serves to contribute to degrowth narratives due to their fundamental critique of hegemonic systems that facilitate climate change. Everingham, for example, elaborates that COVID represents the clearest example of why degrowth is needed. They claim that it has served to highlight the 'unsustainability and fragility of current economic systems', where an outbreak has been able to cause such significant damage to the status quo (Everingham and Chassagne, 2020`). They further elaborate that systemic flaws are exposed in the nature of the recovery that is proposed, by looking at the G7's narrow focus on economic interests on the economy over social well-being and the environment. The G7 elected that "we will work to resolve the health and economic risks caused by the COVID-19 pandemic and set the stage for a strong recovery of strong, sustainable economic growth and prosperity", this serves to bolster degrowth claims that the status quo has limited scope and pursues growth at "any price" (Everingham and Chassagne, 2020).

This viewpoint is shared where other scholars view the pandemic as a catalyst for inviting systemic change and necessary criticism of the status quo. Silva presents the case that COVID has 'opened the potential for a review of our political, economic and social spheres', creating the potential for the advancing the degrowth position that 'aims to reorient values driving political and economic agendas and reward them through lenses of solidarity and care' (Silva, 2020). The context of the crisis has afforded degrowth discursive space, acting as a 'catalyst in the discussions of new paradigms' showing that 'current models are fragile and ill-equipped to challenges, while protecting certain interests over others' (Silva, 2020). This is a point that finds agreement elsewhere, with Mishra noting that the 'pandemic has facilitated urgency leading to calls for a rebooting design of social institutions' (Mishra and Agrawal, 2021). The common theme of literature regarding the exposure of the nature of incumbent systems is to frame it as an opportunity, being a possible midwife of change. This represents the significance of COVID-19 as creating the discursive mobility and impetus for a growing degrowth calls, as Sorokin argues "for good or ill, calamities are unquestionably the supreme disruptors and transformers of social organisation and institutions" (Cohen, 2020). The catalytic capacity of the pandemic, and propensity for exposing flaws in the current order which imbues degrowth proponents with confidence, is seen in that it is 'simultaneously a public health emergency and a real time experiment in downsizing the consumer economy' (Cohen, 2020). The parallels with the 2008 financial crisis must be drawn, where the similar paradigm of potential change was available but ultimately resulting in a swift return to the traditional dominant forces. It must be said that this risk is maintained in the context of the COVID-19 recovery, however, as will be discussed next, there is evidence that overarching global principles are being rejected.

6.2 Retreat of neoliberalism and globalisation

The narrative of degrowth which critiques the vices of the established forces of neoliberalism and globalisation, which have facilitated the dangerous climate crisis, has been able to find success in the pandemic through the retreat of these principles. The crisis has produced policy decisions and action that has undermined the forces of capitalism that had proliferated globally, characterised by increasingly interconnected supply chains, free flows of goods and people and economic dependency. Through the limiting of contact and attempts to stave off the growth of the pandemic, the result can be considered a short-term view at de-globalisation and a retreat of the neoliberal order. We are able to exhibit the change in production and trade habits throughout the crisis that demonstrates this, where there has been a greater 'emphasis on national production and domestic supply' which has seen a reduction in pollution from shipping and aviation (Helm, 2020). Additionally, Everingham eschews to the effects felt on global supply chains, with a shortening of supply chains noted producing the conditions that the degrowth narrative has been promoting, with an increasingly localised and less globally pollutant emphasis on production (Everingham and Chassagne, 2020).

This is significant to the degrowth narrative, as it represents a logistical attempt and experiment, albeit out of necessity, in the degrowing of dominant systems which perpetuate dangerous and pollutant levels of production and consumption. Many of the benefits of such a retreat, which the degrowth movement had outlined prior the pandemic, being environmental benefits and greater resilience to shock, have been demonstrated. As discussed, some had argued that 'globalisation and neoliberal economics was faltering amid multiple strains' in the pre-covid years, but the catalytic effect engendered through crisis seemingly has accelerated the forces which present a case for change and systemic reorganisation (Wells, 2020). However, it must be recognised that this is perhaps a short-term victory for the degrowth narrative. As explored previously, the propensity for the system to reassert itself in the name of recovery has been visible, and in the long term the return to globally interconnected and highly pollutant trade remains highly likely. Despite this, the degrowth narrative has been substantially bolstered through the behavioural shifts practiced throughout, which will be explored next.

6.3 Behaviour and policy

Owing to the substantially transformative capacity of the pandemic, with its ability to impact the way people live, work and operate, there have been further advancements in the degrowth narrative which concern alterations to behaviour and habits which slow the environmental degradation of the planet.

These shifts have been accompanied by policies which have long been lobbied and advocated for by the degrowth movement, and further they represent policy that had long been framed as impossible or impractical in the mainstream prior to the pandemic. Firstly, the attitude and behavioural shifts that were observed are of benefit to the degrowth narrative and serve to counter critics who claim that such communal efforts to solve common problems, like the climate crisis, are unachievable as lifestyles are too embedded. The reality of the COVID-19 pandemic has provided a glimpse into economic and social reorganisation, with the possibility of a 'shift to a service and care economy' away from a hyper consumptive society to living with less (Silva, 2020). This well-being-based economy, which degrowth scholars have long strived for, has been actualised in the reduction of working hours and the demonstration of how important care work is for families, alongside the 'sense of community' which has been fostered in the fight for a common goal (Silva, 2020). The pandemic has proven instrumental in illuminating 'principles of care and solidarity' that have been adopted to protect the health of the majority over the functioning of the economy (Kallis et al, 2020). This common sense of duty and care is a sentiment that contributes to the degrowth narratives, as it contradicts the critiques of behavioural lock in, however the duty and sacrifice demonstrated here, as it was in the example of the Second World War, substantiates the tenets of the narrative.

As well as the progress seen in terms of habitual shifts, which we may say represents the potential for consensus on a change to a well-being economy, there has been significant support demonstrated for the degrowth movement to be a guiding principle of the recovery. A commitment which aims to '1. Put life at the centre of our economic systems, 2. Radically re-evaluate how much and what work is necessary for a good life for all, 3. Organise society around the provision of essential goods and services, 4. Democratise society, 5. Base political and economic systems on the principle of solidarity' has been signed by over

2000 academics and activists during the pandemic (Everingham and Chassagne, 2020). This, alongside the attitude shifts in society, demonstrates that at least at a grassroots level the pandemic has served to embolden calls and capacity for pursuing degrowth.

The enaction of responsive policy to combat the health crisis has also been impactful to the degrowth narrative, illuminating that in reality many of the policy proposals outlined prior to the pandemic are possible and produce positive outcomes. Firstly, we can see that 'global COVID-19 pandemic led to a marked increase in positive discussion of Universal Basic Income' (Nettle et al, 2021) as well as state intervention policies that seek to induce well-being and social protection, such as fewer working hours and rent controls (Everingham and Chassagne, 2020). These policies, although previously marginalised in the neoliberal hegemonic system, have come to the fore in the context of crisis and proven to be successful in that they have manifested environmental and social externalities. This phenomenon is one that is demonstrated through the positive changes to the tourism industry.

The global tourism industry has experienced massive change during the coronavirus pandemic, and resultantly has underscored the ability of the crisis to produce socio-economic shifts which contribute to the development of certain narratives, with. Amrhein discusses the effects of COVID-19 on the tourism industry, which prior to the pandemic had been experiencing 'overtourism', which had 'massively negative impacts' with unlimited tourism taking place (Amrhein, 2022). The phenomenon of COVID-19, however, is now presenting new possibilities for degrowth in the sector where people are calling against a return to 'business as usual' and instead for a move away from its unsustainability which incurs risks to climate change and global health crises (Romagosa, 2020). This is symbolic of the excesses of the status quo and shows the benefits of degrowing sectors, where the halting of unlimited access can produce positive social and environmental outcomes. But it is also able to be countered by arguments of the necessity of jobs in recovery which have been visible previously, where many communities rely heavily on tourism to sustain large parts of their economy and a failure to return tourists to high levels may result in social and economic crises with heavy loss of livelihoods.

Despite this, the examples outlined represent a contradiction of the claims of many critics that degrowth suffers from a lack of precedent and tangible examples, the world has seen a real experiment in downsizing the consumer economy which has seen benefits of varying scales, but ultimately provided the narrative with evidence of the tangibility of many of degrowths proposed policies. Although some have criticised the position of degrowth in the pandemic due to the large negative outcomes of recession, where poverty has been experienced, we can say that this does not represent the aims of the movement, where it instead argues for a managed process in the long term rather than a sudden decline.

7. Conclusion

Overall, to refer back to the comment of Sorokin, that "For good or ill, calamities are unquestionable the supreme disruptors and transformers of social organisation and institutions", it would certainly seem that the COVID-19 pandemic has been representative of this, at least in the short term. The global reach and deep disruptive capacity of the pandemic on established hegemonic practices, systems and logics have been exhibited on a scale before unseen. Degrowth, which has for some time occupied a fringe position, has been thrust into practice and seen many of its arguments and policy proposals put into action, serving to bolster the arguments made by its supporters. Fundamental offerings of degrowth scholars, which seek to attribute growthism and consumption levels with the dangerous levels of emissions have been demonstrably proven right owing to the unavoidable experiment in the downsizing of the consumer economy. Degrowth had capitalised on the initial retreat of the neoliberal and globalised order that was accelerated further in the early stages of the pandemic, where the capacity for a well-being economy which emphasised care and solidarity was possible in order to achieve large scale common goals. This is significant for the fight against climate change, as COVID-19 has illuminated that global solidarity and common will remains available to humanity when the urgency is apparent. The space for an equitable transformation consistent with degrowth goals has been demonstrated by coronavirus, where previously it had not such tangible examples.

However, it must be said that the short-term experience of the pandemic has had significantly different effects to the longer term, which has centred around recovery rather than protection. The emphasis on recovery is where the green growth narrative had been able to achieve substantial progress. Where green growth had already achieved far more progress prior to the pandemic, and was occupying mainstream policy positions and rhetoric, it has been able to assert itself as a dominant socio-economic alternative to the status quo and is now guiding much of the investment and recovery discourse. The dominance of this theory has been attributed to its lack of criticism of the forces of the status quo and growthist logic, and COVID-19 has accelerated this advancement in its narrative that in order to emerge from the pandemic a 'green' recovery must be implored. The previous record of green growth, and the lack of tangibility of its investments made during COVID, represent the environmental populism critiques that have been made prior to the pandemic, where it had achieved far less than it had promised. The pandemic recovery seemingly is being used to justify a consolidation of the existing systems that emphasise more consumption and production, and green growth has further proved itself to be the voice of traditional practices and growth at all costs, even where a slowdown in economic processes has created the environmental effects green growth has promised for over a decade. The long-term impacts of the pandemic had asserted the inability of the degrowth movement to assert itself in the mainstream, that ultimately the imperatives of growth outweighed any of the short-term convivial reorganisations of living. This is indicative of the resilience of neoliberal and globalised economic systems which have been quickly able to return in the name of a 'green recovery'.

The progress of the narratives of alternatives, and resultantly their ability to influence the nature of the response to the climate crisis, is notable. Whether the coronavirus pandemic will operate as a midwife of change, in which the world will see fundamental systemic change and more success in reducing emissions, or a continuation of the forces of old albeit under the disguise of a green veneer, is becoming increasingly clear despite the profound change seen initially in the first few months. Not only this, but the crisis has demonstrated its ability to facilitate shifts backwards, with the investment in highly pollutant industries returning to the fore in the name of the recovery, demonstrating equally that crises have the capacity to produce regression as well as revolution. This then raises the question of whether lessons have been learned from 2008. The current path of recovery would seem to indicate that despite the popular support for well-being policies, common purpose and the benefits of a downturn in consumption and production, that the hegemonic framing of growthism dominates most mainstream recovery rhetoric in the name of saving jobs and livelihoods. The result of this has been an intense rise in emissions to levels higher than before the pandemic, which mirrors the processes that were carried out after the financial crisis. This demonstrates that truly counter systemic proposals for climate alleviation has not achieved mainstream significance yet. However, despite this, the pandemic being a phenomenon like no other has proven possible many systemic, economic, and social changes that were scathed as unrealistic. Combined with this, we see that popular support for climate change action is at its highest, and so through the lens of critical hope it could be said that the behavioural shifts and focus on wellbeing facilitated in the crisis may be the midwife of change in the long-term, but for now the forces of old seem to have returned with force.

Bibliography

Amrhein, S. (2022). Transformative Effects of Overtourism and COVID-19-Caused Reduction of Tourism on Residents—An Investigation of the Anti-Overtourism Movement on the Island of Mallorca. Urban Science, [online] pp.25–25. Available at: https://pesquisa.bvsalud.org/global-literature-on-novel-coronavirus-2019-ncov/resource/fr/covidwho-1765935 [Accessed 3 Aug. 2022].

Antal, M. and Van Den Bergh, J.C.J.M. (2014). Green growth and climate change: conceptual and empirical considerations. Climate Policy, 16(2), pp.165–177. doi:10.1080/14693062.2014.992003.

Asara, V., Otero, I., Demaria, F. and Corbera, E. (2015). Socially sustainable degrowth as a social–ecological transformation: repoliticizing sustainability. Sustainability Science, [online] 10(3), pp.375–384. doi:10.1007/s11625-015-0321-9.

Asara, V., Otero, I., Demaria, F. and Corbera, E. (2015). Socially sustainable degrowth as a social–ecological transformation: repoliticizing sustainability. Sustainability Science, [online] 10(3), pp.375–384. doi:10.1007/s11625-015-0321-9.

Bär, H., Jacob, K. and Werland, S. (2011). [online] Available at:

https://refubium.fu-berlin.de/bitstream/handle/fub188/19914/FFU_Report_07-2011_Baer_Jacob_Werland_Green_Economy-1.pdf [Accessed 3 Aug. 2022].

Bogojević, S. (2020). COVID-19, Climate Change Action and the Road to Green Recovery. Journal of Environmental Law. doi:10.1093/jel/eqaa023.

Bowen, A. and Fankhauser, S. (2011). The green growth narrative: Paradigm shift or just spin? Global Environmental Change, 21(4), pp.1157–1159. doi:10.1016/j.gloenvcha.2011.07.007.

Bowen, A. and Hepburn, C. (2014). Green growth: an assessment. Oxford Review of Economic Policy, [online] 30(3), pp.407–422. Available at: https://www.jstor.org/stable/43664656#metadata_info_tab_contentshttps://www.researchgate.net/publication/272386451_Green_growth_An_assessment [Accessed 3 Aug. 2022].

Bregman, R. (2020). The neoliberal era is ending. What comes next? [online] The Correspondent. Available at: https://thecorrespondent.com/466/the-neoliberal-era-is-ending-what-comes-next.

Büchs, M. and Koch, M. (2019). Challenges for the degrowth transition: The debate about wellbeing. Futures, 105, pp.155–165. doi:10.1016/j.futures.2018.09.002.

Cassidy, J. (2020). Can We Have Prosperity Without Growth? [online] The New Yorker. Available at: https://www.newyorker.com/magazine/2020/02/10/can-we-have-prosperity-without-growth.

Chang, H.-J. (2002). Kicking Away the Ladder: An Unofficial History of Capitalism, Especially in Britain and the United States. Challenge, 45(5), pp.63–97. doi:10.1080/05775132.2002.11034173.

Chomsky, N. and Mcchesney, R.W. (2011). Profit over people : neoliberalism and the global order. New York: Seven Stories Press.

Cohen, M.J. (2020). Does the COVID-19 outbreak mark the onset of a sustainable consumption transition? Sustainability: Science, Practice and Policy, 16(1), pp.1–3.

doi:10.1080/15487733.2020.1740472.

Everingham, P. and Chassagne, N. (2020). Post COVID-19 ecological and social reset: moving away from capitalist growth models towards tourism as Buen Vivir. Tourism Geographies, 22(3), pp.1–12. doi:10.1080/14616688.2020.1762119.

Ferguson, P. (2014). The green economy agenda: business as usual or transformational discourse? Environmental Politics, 24(1), pp.17–37. doi:10.1080/09644016.2014.919748.

Fernando, J. (2022). Globalization. [online] Investopedia. Available at: https://www.investopedia.com/terms/g/globalization.asp.

Fernando, J. (2022). Gross Domestic Product - GDP. [online] Investopedia. Available at: https://www.investopedia.com/terms/g/gdp.asp.

Foster (2011). Capitalism and Degrowth: An Impossibility Theorem. [online] Monthly Review. Available at: https://monthlyreview.org/2011/01/01/capitalism-and-degrowth-an-impossibility-theorem/.

Fukuyama, F. and United States Institute Of Peace (1989). The 'end of history?' Washington, D.C.: United States Institute Of Peace.

Gertney (2010). The New York Times. [online] 13 May. Available at: https://www.nytimes.com/2010/05/16/magazine/16GDP-t.html.

GOV.UK. (2020). COVID-19: background information. [online] Available at: https://www.gov.uk/government/publications/wuhan-novel-coronavirus-background-information.

Gusheva, E. and de Gooyert, V. (2021). Can We Have Our Cake and Eat It? A Review of the Debate on Green Recovery from the COVID-19 Crisis. Sustainability, 13(2), p.874. doi:10.3390/su13020874.

Hanna, R., Xu, Y. and Victor, D.G. (2020). After COVID-19, green investment must deliver jobs to get political traction. Nature, 582(7811), pp.178–180. doi:10.1038/d41586-020-01682-1.

Harvey, F. (2020). US fossil fuel giants set for a coronavirus bailout bonanza. [online] Available at: https://www.theguardian.com/environment/2020/may/12/us-fossil-fuel-companies-coronavirus-bailout-oil-coal-fracking-giants-bond-scheme [Accessed 3 Aug. 2022].

Helm, D. (2020). The Environmental Impacts of the Coronavirus. Environmental and Resource Economics, 76(1), pp.21–38. doi:10.1007/s10640-020-00426-z.

Hepburn, C., O'Callaghan, B., Stern, N., Stiglitz, J. and Zenghelis, D. (2020). Will COVID-19 fiscal recovery packages accelerate or retard progress on climate change? Oxford Review of Economic Policy, 36(1). doi:10.1093/oxrep/graa015.

Hickel, J. and Kallis, G. (2019). Is Green Growth Possible? New Political Economy, [online] 25(4), pp.1–18. doi:10.1080/13563467.2019.1598964.

IEA (2022). Global CO2 emissions rebounded to their highest level in history in 2021 - News. [online] IEA. Available at: https://www.iea.org/news/global-co2-emissions-rebounded-to-their-highest-level-in-history-in-2021.

IMF (n.d.). International Monetary Fund. [online] Available at: https://www.imf.org/-/media/Files/Publications/covid19-special-notes/en-special-series-on-covid-19-greening-the-recovery.ashx10.1093/jel/eqaa023. [Accessed 3 Aug. 2022].

Imperial College London (2020). Resources | Grantham Institute – Climate Change and the Environment | Imperial College London. [online] Available at: https://www.imperial.ac.uk/grantham/publications/a-net-zero-emissions-economic-recovery-from-covid-19.php.

Kallis, G. (2011). In defence of degrowth. Ecological Economics, 70(5), pp.873–880. doi:10.1016/j.ecolecon.2010.12.007.

Kallis, G. (2015). A Great Transition Initiative Viewpoint. [online] Available at: https://greattransition.org/images/Kallis-Degrowth-Alternative.pdf.
Kallis, G., Paulson, S., D'alisa, G. and Demaria, F. (2020). The Case for Degrowth. [online] Polity Press. Available at: http://www.paecon.net/PAEReview/issue93/Morgan93.pdf [Accessed 3 Jun. 2022].

Kuzemko, C. (2020). Covid-19 and the politics of sustainable energy transitions. Energy Research & Social Science, [online] 68, p.101685. doi:10.1016/j.erss.2020.101685.

Mara, L. and Silva, B. (2020). N O V E M B E R 2 0 2 0 V O L U M E 6 T H E C O V I D -1 9 P A N D E M I C A N D T H E D E G R O W T H M O V E M E N T : R E F R A M I N G A N D R E T H I N K I N G E C O N O M I C A N D S O C I A L R E L A T I O N S. [online] Available at: http://www.theopenreview.com/wp-content/uploads/2021/01/Article-9-Borges-Silva-L.M.-COVID-19-Degrowth.pdf [Accessed 3 July. 2022].

Mastini. (2017). Degrowth: the Case for a New Economic Paradigm. [online] Available at: https://www.resilience.org/stories/2017-06-12/degrowth-case-new-economic-paradigm/ [Accessed 2 Jun. 2022].

McCarthy, S. (2020). Lessons from the last recovery for this recovery. [online] Corporate Knights. Available at: https://www.corporateknights.com/leadership/lessons-from-the-last-recovery-for-this-recovery/ [Accessed 3 Aug. 2022].

Mishra, S.N. and Agrawal, A. (2021). Tools of Systemic Change for Sustainable Future: Mindfulness and Degrowth in Post COVID World. [online] papers.ssrn.com. Available at: https://papers.ssrn.com/sol3/papers.cfm?abstract_id=3949533 [Accessed 3 Aug. 2022].

National Geographic Society (2022). Anthropocene | National Geographic Society. [online] education.nationalgeographic.org. Available at: https://education.nationalgeographic.org/resource/anthropocene.

Nettle, D., Johnson, E., Johnson, M. and Saxe, R. (2021). Why has the COVID-19 pandemic increased support for Universal Basic Income? Humanities and Social Sciences Communications, 8(1). doi:10.1057/s41599-021-00760-7.

OECD (2012). OECD Environmental Outlook to 2050: The Consequences of Inaction - Key Facts and Figures - OECD. [online] Oecd.org. Available at: https://www.oecd.org/env/indicators-modelling-outlooks/oecdenvironmentaloutlookto2050theconsequencesofinactionkeyfactsandfigures.htm.

Perkins, P.E. (Ellie) (2019). Climate justice, commons, and degrowth. Ecological Economics, 160, pp.183–190. doi:10.1016/j.ecolecon.2019.02.005.

Peters, G.P., Marland, G., Le Quéré, C., Boden, T., Canadell, J.G. and Raupach, M.R. (2011). Rapid growth in CO2 emissions after the 2008–2009 global financial crisis. Nature Climate Change, 2(1), pp.2–4. doi:10.1038/nclimate1332.

Rashid, T., Pepperrell, T. and Sci, M. (2021). Recentring our economy around wellbeing following the COVID-19 pandemic: A book review of The Case for Degrowth. Journal of Health and Social Sciences Advance Publication Online. [online] doi:10.19204/2021/rcnt7.

Romagosa, F. (2020). The COVID-19 crisis: Opportunities for sustainable and proximity tourism. Tourism Geographies, 22(3), pp.1–5. doi:10.1080/14616688.2020.1763447.

Schneider, F., Kallis, G. and Martinez-Alier, J. (2010). Crisis or opportunity? Economic degrowth for social equity and ecological sustainability. Introduction to this special issue. Journal of Cleaner Production, [online] 18(6), pp.511–518. doi:10.1016/j.jclepro.2010.01.014.

Smith, D.C. (2020). 'Green responses' to COVID-19: Europe and the United States diverge yet again. Journal of Energy & Natural Resources Law, 38(3), pp.209–212. doi:10.1080/02646811.2020.1785766.

Smith, N. (2018). neoliberalism | Definition, Ideology, & Examples. In: Encyclopædia
Britannica. [online] Available at: https://www.britannica.com/topic/neoliberalism.

Sustainable Development Commission (2019). Adoption UK Community. [online] Adoption UK Charity. Available at: https://www.sd-commission.org.uk/pages/what-is-sustainable-development.html.

Taherzadeh, O. (2020). Promise of a green economic recovery post-Covid: trojan horse or turning point? Global Sustainability, pp.1–19. doi:10.1017/sus.2020.33.

Tomaselli, M.F., Kozak, R., Gifford, R. and Sheppard, S.R.J. (2021). Degrowth or Not Degrowth: The Importance of Message Frames for Characterizing the New Economy. Ecological Economics, 183, p.106952. doi:10.1016/j.ecolecon.2021.106952.

United Nations (2020). Everyone included: Social impact of COVID-19. [online] United Nations Department of Economic and Social Affairs. Available at: https://www.un.org/development/desa/dspd/everyone-included-covid-19.html.

United Nations. (2021). World Economic Situation And Prospects: February 2021 Briefing, No. 146. UN News Centre. [online] 6 Feb. Available at: https://www.un.org/development/desa/dpad/publication/world-economic-situation-and-prospects-february-2021-briefing-no-146/.

Wells, P., Abouarghoub, W., Pettit, S. and Beresford, A. (2020). A socio-technical transitions perspective for assessing future sustainability following the COVID-19 pandemic. Sustainability: Science, Practice and Policy, 16(1), pp.29–36. doi:10.1080/15487733.2020.1763002.

World Health Organization: WHO (2019). Climate change - GLOBAL. [online] Who.int. Available at: https://www.who.int/health-topics/climate-change#tab=tab_1.

Zumbrun, J. (2020). World Bank Sees 5.2% Decline in Global Economy in 2020 From Coronavirus. Wall Street Journal. [online] 8 Jun. Available at: https://www.wsj.com/articles/world-bank-sees-5-2-decline-in-global-economy-in-2020-from-coronavirus-11591631209. [Original source: https://studycrumb.com/alphabetizer]